For Warren, Ruby & Jeri. My life, my loves, my heart.
— H.G. / B.D.H.

For my family
— N.D.

THE SOCKEYE MOTHER

By Hetxw'ms Gyetxw (Brett D. Huson)

Illustrated by Natasha Donovan

HIGHWATER
PRESS

SMALL FRY

There's a strong undertow today. The turbulent waters caress the backs of the little semelparous life forms emerging from their gravel nests.[1] A small free-swimming fry[2] bears witness to the currents of spring, after spending weeks developing and using up its nutritious yolk sac. It's one of few remaining fry leaving its long winter's home to seek out nursing waters.

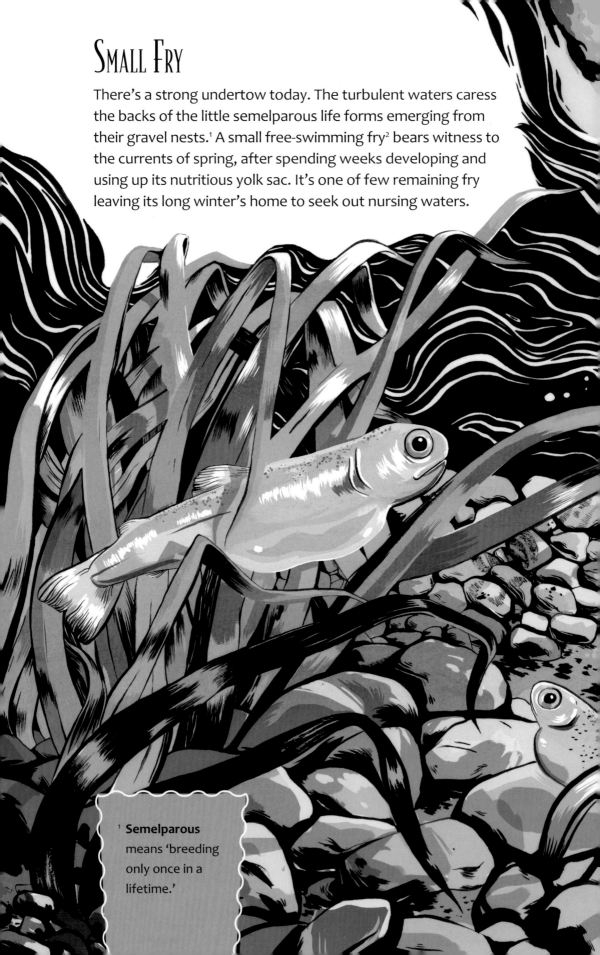

[1] **Semelparous** means 'breeding only once in a lifetime.'

² A **fry** is a recently hatched fish that has reached the stage where it can feed itself. The yolk sac that they fed off has almost disappeared.

This is the time of Wihlaxs (the Black Bear's Walking Moon), which is early spring to the Gitxsan people of the Pacific Northwest Interior. Change is in the air as the days grow longer. Renewal is the life force that guides the world around the little fry's waterways. All flora begin to stir, preparing to bud and bring green to the landscape. Stores of food for the people along Xsan (River of Mists) are running low, but preparations for the new seasons of fishing and gathering have begun. New snow, which the Gitxsan call dalugwa, falls to take away the old snow.

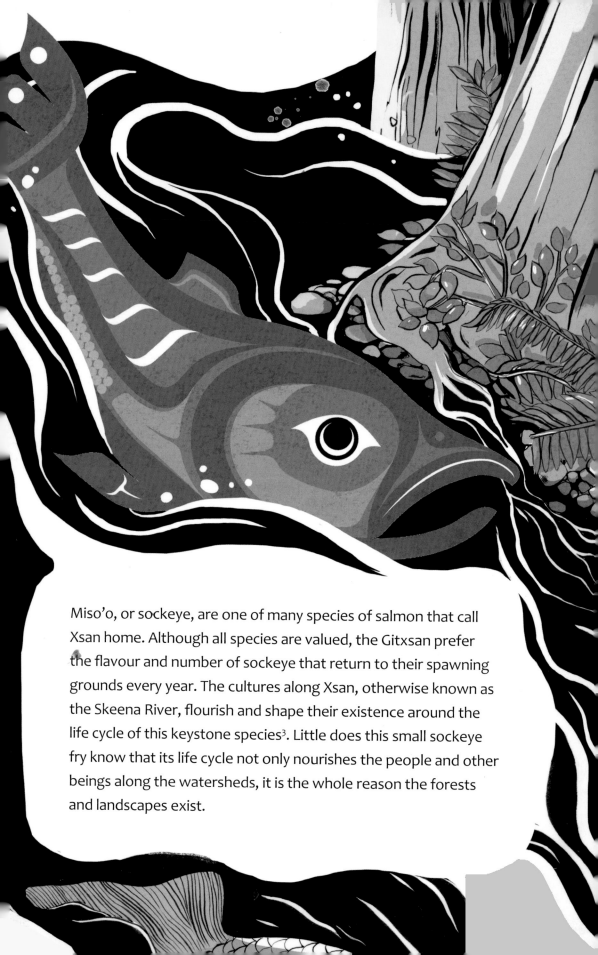

Miso'o, or sockeye, are one of many species of salmon that call Xsan home. Although all species are valued, the Gitxsan prefer the flavour and number of sockeye that return to their spawning grounds every year. The cultures along Xsan, otherwise known as the Skeena River, flourish and shape their existence around the life cycle of this keystone species[3]. Little does this small sockeye fry know that its life cycle not only nourishes the people and other beings along the watersheds, it is the whole reason the forests and landscapes exist.

³ A **keystone** species is a one on which other species in an ecosystem depend.

Time to Grow

After a couple of years of schooling in the deeper parts of the nursing lake, this sockeye has become a smolt.[4] Its little silvery body begins taking the shape of its blue-backed future self. The smolt is outgrowing the lake. This signals Lasa ya'a (the Spring Salmon's Returning Moon), so the little sockeye begins its treacherous journey down the Skeena.

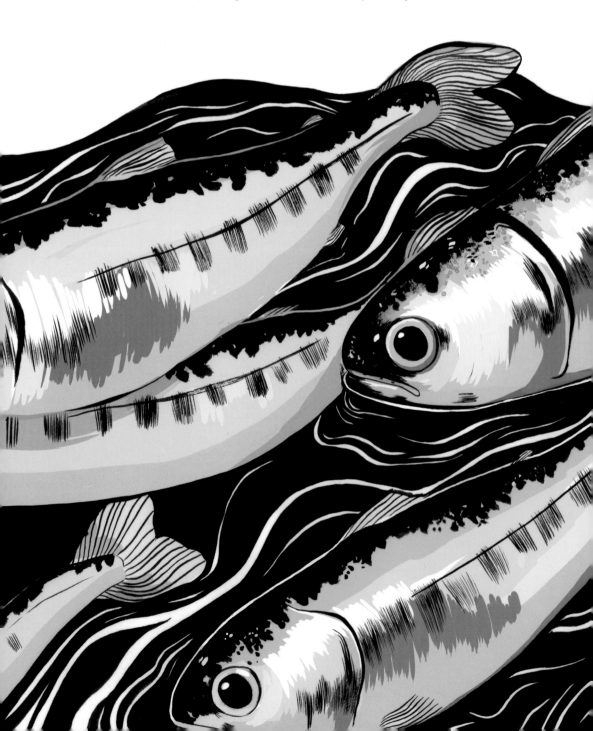

⁴ A **smolt** is a young fish that is undergoing the changes needed to go from living in fresh water to living in salt water.

5 **Saliferous** means 'containing lots of salt.'

As the spring salmons return, the sockeye smolts depart to relieve their urge for saliferous waters.[5] April carries summer innuendos, as warm winds flow through nearly blooming flowers. The scent of pine and cedar wafts across moist, pillowy moss.

The nets and rods of the Gitxsan people scour Xsan in hopes of taking part in the return of ya'a, the spring salmon. Ceremony is held and feasts occur to welcome the runs of salmon who come to replenish the land. It's not only a time to give thanks, but also a time to send prayer that the salmon will always return, that they will provide nourishment for all who are living within its realm.

The young sockeye has so far avoided predators, escaping the hungry hands of 'watxs – the otter – and dodging the unnaturally changing landscape, denuded by the clear-cutting of man. The smolt and her school have made their journey to the Pacific, and north to the ocean waters, where they will continue to feed and grow.

A Replenishing Death

For two years the sockeye mother has been feeding in the ocean waters, while avoiding sharks and killer whales. Through instinct, smell, and much that is still not understood, the sockeye mother swims against the powerful currents of Xsan to return to the exact place in the rivers where she was spawned.[6]

6 **Spawned** means
'released as eggs.'

It's now Lasa lik'i'nxsw (the Grizzly Bear's Moon). August is the time when all the Gitxsan people and grizzly bears pluck hundreds of thousands of sockeye from Xsan. Many predators, such as the grizzly, discard most of the carcass. They carry their catch sometimes hundreds of metres into the forest, only to eat the eggs and fatty bellies. The decaying bodies of the salmon leave nitrogen that nourishes the soil.

Battered and beaten by the journey, the sockeye mother is literally decaying due to constant hard work and lack of food. She finds a male partner who has dug a nest to her liking. She lays her eggs. She can now die a replenishing death. The dying salmon bodies become fertilizer for all the flora that shape the great lands. Without the sockeye mother, the Gitxsan, as they are, would simply not exist.

The Gitxsan

The Gitxsan Nation are indigenous peoples from
their unceded territories of the Northwest Interior
of British Columbia, 35,000 square kilometres of
land that cradles the headwaters of Xsan or "the
River of Mist," also known by its colonial name the
Skeena River. The land defines who they are.

The Nation follows a matrilineal line, and all rights,
privileges, names, and stories come from the mothers.
The fireweed, frog, eagle and wolf are the four clans of the
people. It is taboo to marry a fellow clan member, even when
there are no blood ties.

The four clans are divided among the territories by way of the Wilp
system. A Wilp, or "house group," is a group comprising one or more
families. Each has a head chief and wing chiefs, who are guided by the
members and Elders within the Wilp. Currently, there are 62 house
groups, and each governs their portion of the Gitxsan Territories.

Stekyodin

Bulkley
River

Kispiox
River

Skeena River

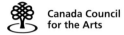
**Canada Council
for the Arts**

We acknowledge the support of the Canada Council for the Arts, which last year invested $153 million to bring the arts to Canadians throughout the country.

Nous remercions le Conseil des arts du Canada de son soutien. L'an dernier, le Conseil a investi 153 millions de dollars pour mettre de l'art dans la vie des Canadiennes et des Canadiens de tout le pays.

HighWater Press gratefully acknowledges the financial support of the Province of Manitoba through the Department of Sport, Culture & and the Manitoba Book Publishing Tax Credit, and the Government of Canada through the Canada Book Fund (CBF), for our publishing activities.

HighWater Press is an imprint of Portage & Main Press.
Printed and bound in Canada by Friesens
Formline drawings by the author
Design by Relish New Brand Experience

This book is based on an article of the same name that appeared in *Red Rising* magazine, May 2016.

Library and Archives Canada Cataloguing in Publication

Huson, Brett D., author
        The sockeye mother / by Hetxw'ms Gyetxw (Brett D. Huson) ; illustrated by Natasha Donovan.

Issued in print and electronic formats.
ISBN 978-1-55379-739-5 (hardcover)
ISBN 978-1-55379-740-1 (ebook)
ISBN 978-1-55379-741-8 (PDF)

    1. Sockeye salmon—Life cycles—Juvenile literature. 2. Sockeye salmon—British Columbia—Juvenile literature. 3. Gitxsan Indians—British Columbia—Juvenile literature. I. Donovan, Natasha, illustrator II. Title.

QL638.S2H87 2017   j597.5'6   C2017-905976-9
                                             C2017-905977-7

20 19 18 17   1 2 3 4 5

HIGHWATER PRESS

www.highwaterpress.com
Winnipeg, Manitoba
Treaty 1 Territory and homeland of the Métis Nation.